3 0063 00284 5560

Main   July 2018

DISCARD

THIS CANDLEWICK BOOK BELONGS TO:

_____

_____

_____

D1361185

For Lucy I., Val C., and Julia G.
N. D.

For Will and his generosity
N. L.

Text copyright © 2007 by Nicola Davies
Illustrations copyright © 2007 by Neal Layton

All rights reserved. No part of this book may be reproduced, transmitted, or stored in an information retrieval system in any form or by any means, graphic, electronic, or mechanical, including photocopying, taping, and recording, without prior written permission from the publisher.

First U.S. paperback edition 2009

The Library of Congress has cataloged the hardcover edition as follows:
Davies, Nicola, date.
What's eating you? : parasites — the inside story / Nicola Davies ; illustrated by Neal Layton. —1st U.S. ed.
p.   cm.
ISBN 978-0-7636-3460-5 (hardcover)
1. Parasites — Juvenile literature. I. Layton, Neal, ill. II. Title.
QL757D38 2007
591.6'5 — dc22   2007025634
ISBN 978-0-7636-4521-2 (paperback)

17 18 TWP 10 9 8 7

Printed in Malaysia

This book was typeset in AT Arta.
The illustrations were done in ink and digitally colored.

Candlewick Press
99 Dover Street
Somerville, Massachusetts 02144

visit us at www.candlewick.com

THE CHIMPANZEE ON THE OPPOSITE PAGE IS ABOUT TO EAT A **BIG** BUNCH OF SPIKY LEAVES. YOU CAN FIND OUT WHY IF YOU TURN TO PAGE 46...

DAVENPORT PUBLIC LIBRARY
321 MAIN STREET
DAVENPORT, IOWA 52801

What's **Eating** You?

Parasites – the Inside Story

Nicola Davies

illustrated by **Neal Layton**

GULP!

CANDLEWICK PRESS

Up a tree or down a hole,

out to sea or in a puddle,

somewhere hot or somewhere cold . . .

every animal has a habitat, a place where it belongs,
a place where it can find food and shelter and have its babies.

You Are a Habitat!

But there is a group of creatures
whose habitats are not forests or seas or deserts. They live on or in the bodies of other animals.
Their habitats are skin and hair, fur and feathers, blood and guts, livers and hearts and lungs.
They are called parasites, and there are an awful lot of them. In fact, some scientists think
that there are more kinds of parasites than there are of any other sort of animal.

Almost every free-living animal on the planet is just a walking habitat — a "host" to many parasites —
and that includes us humans! There are more than 430 different kinds of parasites that can live on
a human body (ectoparasites) or in one (endoparasites).

Don't panic! Modern humans are too clean and well cared for to have lots of parasites. You
certainly don't have 430 different kinds! But you just may have one or two, even if you think you
don't. That's because although some parasites make their hosts feel rather ill, others don't do
any harm at all, and you would never know you were being used as a habitat. But you *mite*
find out about those later! (There's a clue there. Just wait and see.)

Meet Some Ectoparasites . . .

(They live outside the body.)

Parasites LOVE **purple martins**! Louse flies and four different kinds of bird lice eat their blood; feather mites eat their feathers; and quill mites live in their feathers and eat their skin.

The rare **greater naked bat** has five different unusual parasites—five different kinds of parasitic earwigs, including one nearly an inch long!

Slippery skin doesn't keep parasites away. Several kinds of flies lay their eggs on **frogs** so that their maggots can eat the frogs' flesh! And frogs get leeches, too.

And Meet Some Endoparasites . . .

(They live inside the body.)

Purple martins have mites in their lungs, as well as roundworms and thorny-headed worms in their guts.

Parasites on parasites! Fly maggots feed on the blood of nesting martins, and tiny wasps lay their eggs on the fly maggots.

Greater naked bats are so rare that no one's looked inside them yet, but they probably have tapeworms, roundworms, and hookworms, just as other kinds of bats do.

Parasites live in almost every part of a **frog's** insides: flatworms in the lungs, roundworms in the gut, and a special kind of flatworm that can live only in the frog's bladder.

What Makes a Good Parasite?

A GOOD PARASITE

Polar bears need thick coats to beat the cold, and giraffes need long necks to reach their food. But parasites need to be much smarter than ordinary animals to survive in their body habitats.

First, they need to be small: it's no good being the size of an elephant if your habitat is the fur of a mouse. And second, they need to be super-adaptable, because finding a host can be very different from living on it or in it, so being able to change body shape is a big advantage to a parasite.

Most vertebrates — birds, mammals, reptiles, amphibians, and fish — can't be parasites; they're just too big, and their bodies are set in one form. But invertebrate animals, like insects, worms, snails, and single-celled animals, are small and can change their body shape and form during their lives (think of caterpillars turning into butterflies). So some of them make really good parasites and can adapt to life on and off their chosen host in mind-bogglingly amazing ways.

THE PARASITE CLUB

MEMBERS ONLY
NO MAMMALS
OR BIG FISH

Getting Aboard

Living bodies are not the easiest places to live. They do things that other habitats don't do. For a start, they move around, so the first problem a parasite has to solve is how to get onto its habitat and stay there. Since most hosts are much bigger and faster than their parasites, this can seem as impossible as a mouse trying to hitch a ride on a jumbo jet. Yet parasites manage it all the time.

The most basic approach to host-hitching is to hang around and hope that one will pass by. This is what ticks do. These little bloodsucking relatives of spiders stay on their hosts only long enough to get a meal. They climb into grass and bushes, and when they smell an animal close by, they wave their legs to grab a ride.

This hit-or-miss method often works, because ticks aren't picky eaters — any warm-blooded animal will do, humans included — and they don't need to hang on for long. As soon as they've had their blood meal and have swollen from pinhead to fat-baked-bean size, they drop back into the grass to lay eggs.

Most fleas don't live on their hosts full-time, either. They start life as larvae, living in the host's bed. When the adult fleas hatch, they rely on warmth or movement to tell them there's a body nearby, and then they start leaping . . . and leaping . . . and leaping. They can keep leaping for hours on end — jumping up to one hundred times their own body length, which is like a person jumping over the Eiffel Tower! With luck, this will bring the flea into contact with a host. Then it can grab ahold and wriggle down into the jungle of fur or feathers. If anything tries to pull it out, the flea is covered in backward-pointing spines that tangle in the host's coat and hold it fast.

AFTER ALL THAT, I'M STAYING PUT!

There are lots of kinds of fleas, and they all have a favorite host. But the big-leap method of host-finding is a bit unreliable (you can't be sure what you'll jump onto), so most fleas are able to get a meal from more than one kind of animal. Cat fleas, for example, find humans quite tasty, and human fleas will bite dogs, pigs, and even burrowing owls!

WANTED: TASTY HOST

HUNGRY FLEA SEEKS A HOST. NOT FUSSY. ANY CAT, PIG, OR BURROWING OWL WILL DO.

Staying Aboard

One way to avoid getting onto the wrong host is never to get off the right one. Parasites that do this have to become experts at living on one kind of host — so good, in fact, that they *can't* live anywhere else.

Rabbit fleas never leave their bunny hosts; they even breed at the same time as their bunnies. When baby rabbits are born, the fleas move from Mom to babies. They lay their eggs on the babies, then move back to Mom. But newly hatched flea grubs can't suck blood, so before the adult fleas return to Mother Rabbit, they make food for their offspring — a load of their own poop, especially rich in bunny blood, for the grubs to munch on. This way, adults and young fleas get everything they need aboard their rabbit world.

Human hair mites get all they need from their hosts — us! They are tiny relatives of spiders, about one-tenth of a millimeter long (smaller than a grain of salt), with bodies like miniature salamis and four

A SUPER-ENLARGED DRAWING OF A HUMAN HAIR MITE

0.1 mm

(WHICH IS REALLY, REALLY, REALLY SMALL)

pairs of stumpy legs. They live in the roots of hair (usually eyelashes or eyebrows), where they munch on dead skin and sebum (the oily stuff that keeps hair shiny). The only time they wander is when young mites search for a hair of their own, when they may find their way onto another body.

DEAD SKIN AND SEBUM! MY FAVORITE!

You *might* have mites without knowing. (Remember that clue?) Your grandma almost certainly does, because your chances of getting mites go up with age. But don't worry; they're harmless.

COME AND GIVE YOUR GRANDMA AND HER HAIR MITES A BIG HUG!

Lice: The Stay-at-Home Specialists

You certainly would know about it if you had lice. Their bites would make your skin itch, and if you had a lot of lice, you might even feel tired and sick — "lousy," in fact.

Human head lice, otherwise known as "cooties," are so good at living on our hair that they can't live anywhere else. They are tiny (less than 1.5 millimeters long), so they can hide easily, and they have claws exactly the right size to grab human head hair. They are incredibly tough and can survive hair washing with no difficulty at all. Even if you manage to wash out the grown-ups, the eggs (commonly called nits) survive.

The Louse Family

The stay-at-home tactics of lice have let them specialize in living on one type of host or even one part of a host. There are lice that live only on birds' *wings* and others that live only on their *heads*; there are lice that live only on guinea pigs and lice that live only on seals. In fact, lice have been so successful that there are 3,000 different kinds.

Legless, Eyeless, Mouthless . . . and Ready!

Parasites that live on the insides of bodies — endoparasites — are even more specialized than the most specialized stay-at-home louse. They may not have legs, eyes, or even mouths and guts, because inside another body, they don't need them. So endoparasites can look seriously weird.

The human tapeworm, for instance, looks like a visitor from another planet. Tapeworms can live in your intestine and grow to 60 feet long! Their bodies are shaped like a tape measure and are made of hundreds of little flattened segments. Instead of a head, they have a thing called a scolex, a kind of knob with a series of hooks and suckers on it that holds on to the inside of the intestine. They don't have eyes, because there's no light to see with inside an intestine, and they don't have legs, because they don't go anywhere. They don't need a mouth or a gut of their own, because they just float around in your digested food and soak it up through their skin.

There are plenty of other wormy parasites that can live in your guts: whipworms, like bits of spaghetti; roundworms as big as your finger, and tiny threadlike pinworms — all swimming in your food. And there are hookworms, which don't feed on your *food*, but feed on *you*, munching intestines and blood.

SCOLEX

TAPEWORM

TAPE MEASURE

Sneaking In

The question is, how do these animals get into your intestine? Obviously you'd notice if you were swallowing a 60-foot tapeworm or even a couple of little pinworms. This is where the common invertebrate trick of morphing from one body form to another comes in handy for parasites. They get into your body as teeny eggs or larvae, then change into their grown-up selves!

Pinworms, for example, get into you as eggs. The adult worm pokes out of its host's bottom at night to lay eggs on the skin just outside. The eggs are so tiny and light that they can just blow all over a house, including into mouths, without anyone noticing. The pinworm eggs get swallowed and hatch when they reach the gut.

28

Hookworm eggs are squeezed out with their host's poop, but because humans don't eat their own poop (some animals do — rabbits, for instance!), hookworms need some other route into a new body. So . . . the eggs hatch into baby hookworms tiny enough to wiggle between human skin cells, and in places where poop can be stepped into by people, they get into the blood and then back to the gut — where they grow up and start feeding.

AW! ISN'T HE CUTE!

MAMA!

TINY BABY HOOKWORM

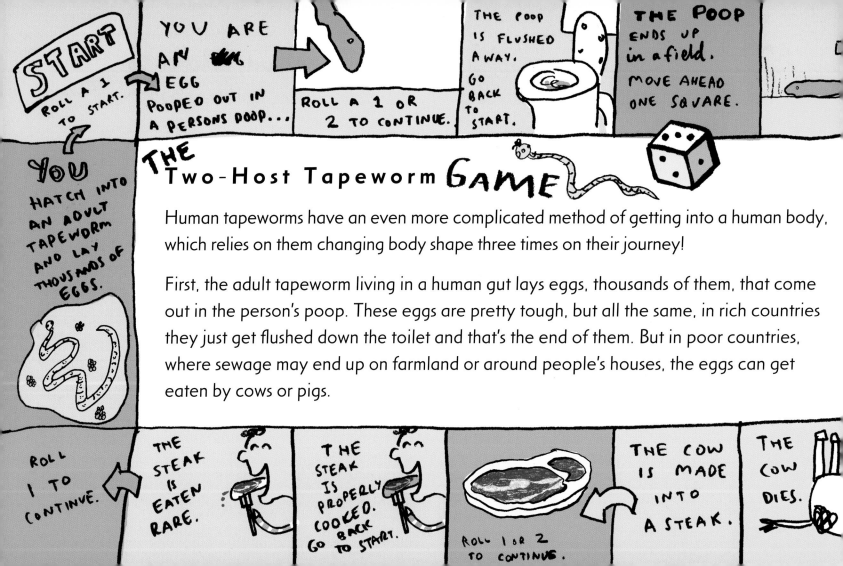

START ROLL A 1 TO START.

YOU ARE AN ~~EGG~~ EGG POOPED OUT IN A PERSONS POOP...

ROLL A 1 OR 2 TO CONTINUE.

THE POOP IS FLUSHED AWAY. GO BACK TO START.

THE POOP ENDS UP in a field. MOVE AHEAD ONE SQUARE.

YOU HATCH INTO AN ADULT TAPEWORM AND LAY THOUSANDS OF EGGS.

THE Two-Host Tapeworm GAME

Human tapeworms have an even more complicated method of getting into a human body, which relies on them changing body shape three times on their journey!

First, the adult tapeworm living in a human gut lays eggs, thousands of them, that come out in the person's poop. These eggs are pretty tough, but all the same, in rich countries they just get flushed down the toilet and that's the end of them. But in poor countries, where sewage may end up on farmland or around people's houses, the eggs can get eaten by cows or pigs.

ROLL 1 TO CONTINUE.

THE STEAK IS EATEN RARE.

THE STEAK IS PROPERLY COOKED. GO BACK TO START.

ROLL 1 OR 2 TO CONTINUE.

THE COW IS MADE INTO A STEAK.

THE COW DIES.

THE POOP IS EATEN BY A COW.

ROLL ~~SEVEN~~ 1 TO HATCH.

Well done! You have hatched out into a little hooked BLOB.

Inside a pig or a cow, they hatch into little hooked blobs, which wiggle into the blood and ride around until they get to a muscle. There they change again, into an egg-shaped bubble called a bladder worm. (See? Told you it was complicated!)

The tapeworm can only grow up and lay eggs in a human, not in a cow or a pig. So the bladder worm has to wait . . . and wait . . . and wait . . . until the cow or pig becomes some unlucky person's undercooked beef or pork dinner. The worm slips down with the meat, then pops out of its bubble. Now, at last, it can settle down, turn into an adult, and lay eggs.

ROLL A 1 TO FIND A MUSCLE.

MOVE AHEAD ONE SQUARE.

YOU TURN INTO A BLADDER WORM.

Roll a 1 to turn into a bladder worm.

YOU FIND A MUSCLE. MOVE AHEAD ONE SQUARE.

The Host Is Toast!

Many different kinds of tapeworms use this weird route, getting to the host in which they can breed (called a "primary host") via a host in which they can't breed (a "secondary host"). This is good news for the primary host, since the tapeworm tries not to hurt it, because it wants to stay and breed for as long as possible. But it is very bad news indeed for the secondary host, because the tapeworm wants the secondary host to be eaten as soon as possible. And tapeworms have creepy ways of getting what they want. Here are a couple of examples. . . .

32   A tapeworm of herons travels via a little secondary-host fish called a stickleback. How does the tapeworm get from fish to heron? By turning the fish orange or white and making it swim so close to the surface of the water that a hunting heron couldn't possibly miss it.

Wolf tapeworms stop off in their secondary host, the moose. The tapeworm makes sure it gets to its favorite host—the wolf—by making the moose easy to catch: it gets into the moose's lungs, making its breath smelly and wheezy. So the moose is easy to find and can't run very fast!

And there are many similar stories where the secondary host ends up as the toast of the primary host.

SNIFF ← PRIMARY HOST

SECONDARY HOST →

PUFF... WHEEZE...

Deadly Delivery

Getting eaten seems like a pretty direct route into another animal's body, but there are parasites so sm[all] that they can get themselves injected into the blood of their host in the bite of an insect.

If someone asked you what is the most dangerous animal in the world, what would you choose? A tige[r?] A grizzly bear? A poisonous snake? All wrong. The deadliest creature on the planet — apart from humans, of course — is so very small, you'd need a microscope to see it. It's called plasmodium and is delivered in the bite of a mosquito.

Millions of plasmodia wait inside a mosquito's mouth until it bites a human. Then they rush down the mosquito's needle-like mouthparts and into the blood. Once in, plasmodia are tiny enough to hide inside a single cell — the body's smallest building block. Each plasmodium makes a cell its slave, using up the cell's energy to make copies of itself, then casting it aside like an empty bag of potato chips. In two weeks, each plasmodium has made 640,000 copies of itself.

People with this going on inside are very sick indeed. They have the disease we call malaria, which kills one million people every year, mostly in warm, wet, tropical countries where mosquitoes are common.

Kill or Cure

As far as the parasite plasmodium is concerned, the host is just a pantry. But it must make sure that some of its copies escape before the host dies. So the plasmodium parasites call their mosquito taxi to come and get them by making infected people smell extra nice (actually like cheesy feet!) to mosquitoes. The mosquito bites, sucks up blood with plasmodium parasites in it, then flies off, ready to bite someone else and give the parasite a new host to live in.

36 Where there are lots of people and lots of mosquitoes, this is really easy, so it doesn't matter to the plasmodium if it kills its host — fast. But where getting out to another host could take time — where there are fewer people or mosquitoes — the plasmodium must be nicer and not make its host so sick. The host may even recover from malaria but go on carrying plasmodium parasites in its blood all its life.

← LOTS OF MOSQUITOES

← NOT SO MANY MOSQUITOES

Parasite Mind Control

Although a plasmodium may make its host very sick (and make it smell like old socks), it doesn't tell the host what to do. But there are plenty of parasites clever enough to control their host as if it were a puppet and the parasite were pulling the strings.

Sacculina is a sea-living relative of crabs. It starts life as a swimming larva, like a tiny shrimp. But as soon as it meets a crab, it shrugs off its whole body and injects a minute blob of cells into the crab. These grow tentacles into every single part of the crab's body, even its brain, to control everything it does. The crab is now just *Sacculina*'s slave. It eats but doesn't grow, because all its food now feeds *Sacculina*. It doesn't breed but rears *Sacculina*'s babies instead, as though they were its own. Even male crabs do this: *Sacculina* makes males behave like females with babies.

Parasitic flies can control bumblebees' brains and even make them get into their own graves. The flies inject eggs into the bee's body so that the larvae, when they hatch, can eat the bee alive. The larvae want the bee to stay somewhere safe and out of sight so it won't get eaten, so they send a message to the bee's brain. This makes the bee crawl into a hole and cover itself up before dying.

Horsehair worms are parasites that keep their grasshopper hosts healthy until they are ready to return to the water. Then they make the grasshopper want to jump into water, where the worms can break out, leaving the broken body of the grasshopper behind.

Good Grooming Could Save Your Life!

By now you may be feeling rather uncomfortable, even a bit sick, at the thought of parasites using your body as their property. Get ready to feel better. The good news is that there is a lot that we, and other animals, can do to fight back.

Ectoparasites, like ticks, fleas, and lice, can weaken an animal and make it easy prey, so good grooming can mean the difference between life and death. Grooming — with teeth and beaks, paws and claws — can do a really good job of combing out and squishing up to 90 percent of parasites. But it needs to be done regularly — some animals spend up to six hours every day grooming. What's more, many also groom each other to make sure that awkward spots they can't reach themselves are kept parasite-free.

This I'll-scratch-your-back-if-you-scratch-mine approach is an important part of animal social life. Grooming the back of your mate's head shows affection in birds. In gorillas, who-grooms-whom is a status symbol, so the top male in the group gets groomed by everyone.

Parasite-popping is so important for kangaroos that they have built-in grooming equipment: two of their toes are stuck together to make a two-clawed grooming tool.

SPECIAL GROOMING TOOL

← SPECIAL GROOMING TOOL

A ROO'S FOOT

A HERON

A HERON'S TOE

Barn owls and herons have a comb on their middle toe to help scrape lice off their feathers.

Impalas tempt ticks into a place where they can get them with their teeth by having black stripes on their bottoms! Ticks go for warmth, so they huddle up in the warm black fur — just where the impala's teeth can reach them.

GOTCHA!

Starlings use strong-smelling plants in their nests to keep parasites off their babies.

Birds can use chemicals to get rid of parasites. Hoopoes make smelly oil in their preen gland (on the tail) to spread over their feathers and put off parasites. Some jays even pick up ants and use the acid from their stings to kill lice.

American screech owls, though, may have found the best anti-louse treatment of all: they keep a small insect-eating snake in their nests!

Sea creatures living on tropical reefs can "go to the cleaners" to get rid of parasites. Little striped fish called cleaner wrasses specialize in biting the parasites off other fish and turtles. The wrasses show they are ready to do some cleaning by swimming around, wriggling their stripy bodies. Animals with parasites then line up and wait their turn to be cleaned. The wrasses get a tummy full of juicy parasites as payment for their services!

Take Your Medicine . . . Like a Chimp!

Chimps have found a way to comb their insides for parasitic worms: they swallow bunches of spiky leaves, which pull the worms from their intestines like sticky Velcro. Chimps also take medicine. They swallow the bitter pith of a forest plant that kills worms. (And they make the same faces as we do when we take nasty cough medicine!) In fact, scientists are only just beginning to discover how many animals eat particular plants as medicine to get rid of parasites. Even some caterpillars do it; when they have the eggs of parasitic flies inside them, caterpillars switch to eating poisonous leaves to help them survive!

46   We humans have invented all sorts of medicines to kill harmful parasites inside our bodies and the bodies of our animals. The problem is that parasites get used to medicines and then stop dying. Whenever scientists invent a new way of killing a parasite, the parasite just comes up with a new way to survive. That's why head lice are doing so well and why malaria is still killing so many people. It's a constant battle; sometimes the parasites are in the lead, and sometimes we are.

Breaking the Circle

Medicines aren't always the best way to defeat a parasite. The complicated body-morphing life cycles of some parasites make them easy to attack with a little bit of knowledge.

The guinea worm is a 2-foot-long worm that likes to wander around a human body until it gets to a leg. It makes a hole in the leg, which is sore and painful, and the only way the human host can make it feel better is by wading in cold water. This is just what the guinea worm wants. It releases its tiny babies through the hole into the water, where they get inside the bodies of mini shrimp-type animals called copepods. When a person swallows a copepod in his or her drinking water, the guinea worm babies leave the shrimp and start their wanderings through another human body all over again.

Three and a half million people, from Africa to India, used to have to put up with guinea worms. But now people filter their drinking water, so they don't swallow any copepods with baby guinea worms inside. Simple as that. The guinea worm is now on its way to being an endangered species, all because of a little bit of knowledge.

Built-in Defense

Breaking the links in a parasite's life cycle will eventually finish it off. But even without the help of knowledge or medicine, animals and humans have a built-in defense system to protect them against parasites that get inside their bodies. It's called the immune system, and in mammals like us humans, it works extremely well.

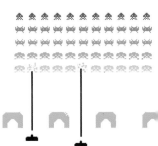

The immune system is made up of millions and millions of tiny cells that patrol all parts of your body like soldiers on the lookout for invaders — from big parasites like worms to tiny ones like plasmodia. These cells don't have eyes or ears, but they can recognize any parasite by the pattern of chemicals on its skin; then they attack. The immune cells can mass together, dissolve the parasite's skin, and eat it, or they can set up a fever, which makes the body so hot that the parasite can't survive.

Parasites can get around the immune system by disguising themselves or changing so fast that the immune system doesn't recognize them, or by hiding inside a host's own cells — as plasmodia do. Most of the time, though, the immune system wins, and you never even know about the invaders it has been fighting for you.

50

I'm Only Marrying You for Your Immune System....

Immune systems and parasites have been battling away in human bodies for many thousands of years. Right now, this minute, your immune system is fighting invaders you'll never even know about. Without your immune system, you'd die. In fact, your immune system is so important that one day it might tell you whom to marry!

Scientists have found that, when humans are choosing their mates, people prefer partners with immune systems that have the pieces that their own systems lack, so that any children they have together will be even better at fighting parasites.

But how do you know? Apparently someone with a complementary immune system just smells nice to you!

WHY DON'T WE GET TOGETHER?

SMELLS LIKE A GOOD IDEA!

THE IMMUNE SYSTEM

A PIECE THAT THE IMMUNE SYSTEM LACKS

Planet Parasite

You mustn't go away with the idea that parasites are all bad, because as we humans find out more about them, we discover ways in which they can help us, not just harm us.

Some crop pests, for example, can be controlled with parasites, so farmers don't have to use toxic chemicals, which might kill other wildlife, too. Mealybugs that were destroying cassava, the most important food crop in Africa, were killed off by bringing in a little wasp that is a parasite of mealybugs.

Parasites can even cure diseases. Conditions like allergies and bowel disease can be helped by giving sufferers a controlled dose of parasitic worms. Although scientists are not yet sure why this works, it could be that humans actually *need* parasites. It certainly looks as if parasites are a vital part of nature — from whole habitats to single cells. Scientists studying tropical forests have found that plenty of parasites is a sign that a jungle is doing well. Almost every cell in every plant and animal contains tiny grains called mitochondria that act like batteries, giving the cells energy. These mitochondria invaded the first cells millions of years ago as parasites, and became essential parts of every living thing.

Humans are only beginning to understand the ways in which parasites have shaped life on Earth. They are not just villains, but an amazing group of animals that have evolved complex and inventive ways of surviving in their chosen habitats.

One thing's for sure: a planet without parasites would be a lot less interesting!

Parasite Champions!

Biggest: Blue whales are the largest animals on the planet, so their tapeworms are BIG — up to 90 feet long.

Bravest: a little copepod that lives between the teeth of the fiercest predator in the ocean, the great white shark.

58

Hello!!

Weirdest: a copepod called Cymothoa that eats a fish's tongue, then lives inside its mouth, acting as a replacement tongue.

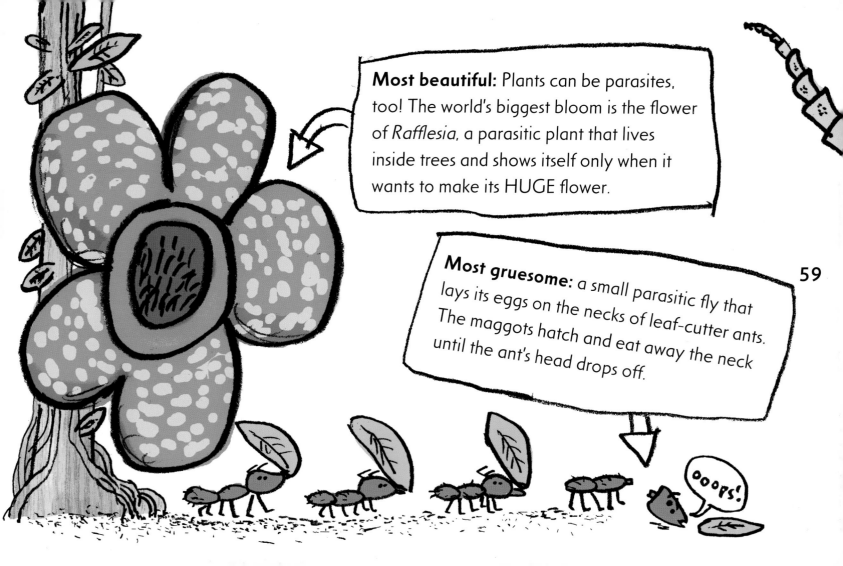

Most beautiful: Plants can be parasites, too! The world's biggest bloom is the flower of *Rafflesia*, a parasitic plant that lives inside trees and shows itself only when it wants to make its HUGE flower.

Most gruesome: a small parasitic fly that lays its eggs on the necks of leaf-cutter ants. The maggots hatch and eat away the neck until the ant's head drops off.

59

ooops!

INDEX

GLOSSARY

ectoparasite a parasite that lives on the outside of a body (up noses and in ears still count as outside)

endoparasite a parasite that lives inside a body, including in the gut or organs or blood

habitat the sort of place where an animal or plant lives. Gorillas' habitat is the rain forest; the habitat of sidewinder snakes is the desert.

host the animal or plant that a parasite lives on or in; its habitat

immune system millions of cells devoted to protecting a body from parasites both large and teeny

invertebrate an animal without a skeleton on the inside. Worms, insects, shrimp, and squid are all invertebrates; fish, amphibians, reptiles, birds, and mammals aren't.

mitochondria tiny parts of a cell that help it to burn food and make energy for life

primary host the host that the parasite breeds in

secondary host the host that the parasite doesn't breed in

vertebrate an animal with a skeleton on the inside. Amphibians, reptiles, birds, mammals, and fish are all vertebrates.

Nicola Davies is a zoologist and writer whose many acclaimed nonfiction books for children include *Surprising Sharks*, *Ice Bear*, *Poop*, and *Extreme Animals*. She says, "My dad was a trained biologist and keen amateur naturalist. Whenever he found any dead animal, he took the opportunity to give me a lesson in dissection, so together we ran into all sorts of endoparasites. I always wondered what their lives were like in that strange, warm, dark world that is inside all of us!"

Neal Layton has illustrated more than forty books for children, including *Poop* and *Extreme Animals*. He says, "My favorite page in the book is probably the two-host tapeworm game. If you have dice and a couple of counters, you can actually play it and follow the life cycle of a tapeworm from tiny egg to adult worm. Fascinating and fun!"